Healing Feelings Series

The Sprinklets & Pestlets Take Over Earth

Adventure Two

By Patrice Joy, MA

Illustrated by Kristen Croxton, BA

Healing Feelings Series: The Sprinklets & Pestlets Take Over Earth – Adventure Two
Copyright © 2019 by Patrice Joy Harkins - Heartlink Creations

All rights reserved.
This book or any portion thereof may not be reproduced or used in any manner whatsoever without the express written permission of the publisher except for the use of brief quotations in a book review.

ISBN 978-1-7325939-1-6

Library of Congress Control Number: 2018910

Editors: Alida Coughlin, C. J. Wright

Illustrator: Kristen Croxton

Printed in the United States of America
First Printing, 2019

Printed by KDP
Available from Amazon.com, CreateSpace.com, and other retail outlets

Published by Heartlink Creations
Bedford, KY

Inquiries: healingfeelings333@gmail.com

Acknowledgement

I want to thank my family and friends for the exciting adventures that are incorporated in the Healing Feelings Series. The contents of these were taken from times we shared as they were growing up. The sprinklets and pestlets and puppets were the basis of learning moral values and the power of positive interactions. My family, including five sons Brent, Trevor, Ed, Patrick and Kevin; daughter Lisa; eight grandchildren Tara, Heather, Savannah, Matthew, Cory, Dylan, Elliott, and Abe; and three great granddaughters Ava, Leah and Natalie gave the inspiration for these stories. I am grateful for my four daughters in law, Cindy, Anne, Julie and Shannon and my soul granddaughter, Paige.

Thanks to my 'soul sisters' in the Native Women's Wisdom Circle who have been there for me through thick and thin. My friends Joy, Carol, Carla, Donna, Leslie, Deb and Angela shared love and faith to encourage me. I will always hold Momfeather, Pat, Koon Dog, Amy and Bev most dear in my heart through time.

I offer special thanks to my son Ed and my husband Dan who helped a great deal with the editing and publishing process. I am grateful for the talented illustrators, Kristen and Nancy, who have brought my stories to life in color and form; and for my loyal friends Alida, CJ and the publishers. Without all of you, I couldn't have finished this project.

OpenDyslexic font is more easily read by persons with some common symptoms of dyslexia.

Permission is hereby granted, free of charge, to any person obtaining a copy of the fonts accompanying this license ("Fonts") and associated documentation files (the "Font Software"), to reproduce and distribute the Font Software, including without limitation the rights to use, copy, merge, publish, distribute, and/or sell copies of the Font Software, and to permit persons to whom the Font Software is furnished to do so, subject to the following conditions:

The above copyright and trademark notices and this permission notice shall be included in all copies of one or more of the Font Software typefaces.

The Font Software may be modified, altered, or added to, and in particular the designs of glyphs or characters in the Fonts may be modified and additional glyphs or characters may be added to the Fonts, only if the fonts are renamed to names not containing either the words "Bitstream" or the word "Vera."

This License becomes null and void to the extent applicable to Fonts or Font Software that has been modified and is distributed under the "Bitstream Vera" names. OpenDyslexic by Bitstream Vera is a trademark of Bitstream, Inc.

We invite you to enjoy the games, puppet shows and learning activities in Book Five. They are designed to increase your fun and help you understand and control your feelings. Experience meeting the Sprinklets personally with relaxing imagery and color.

See full series and other books by Patrice Joy

Healing Feelings Series

    Book 1: Meet the Sprinklets & Pestlets
    Book 2: The Sprinklets & Pestlets Take Over Earth
    Book 3: Teddy the Turtle's Family & Friends
    Book 4: Teddy, Bonnie & the Bullies
    Book 5: Play Potentials Booklet
    Book 6: Practical Life Skills & Related Research

Pet Adventures

    Book 1: Buffy Meets Lucky
    Book 2: Friends Forever

Dolphins Dreaming

Feather Friends

Self Awareness Sprinklet & Pestlet Cards

Introduction

**The content in this Healing Feeling Adventure is designed
for those in elementary school and older
to understand the consequences of their thoughts and feelings.
It's also meant to reach the 'inner child' in those of all ages.**

    'The Sprinklets and Pestlets Take Over Earth' tells what can happen when a Fearful Pestlet takes over. People start to think only of themselves and how much they can get from others. They don't want to share, and they don't care about love. They believe that having lots of things and tons of money will make them happy. Some people feel this is necessary to be safe.

    Cultural, environmental and social changes cause many people to fear there won't be enough resources on Earth like food, water and even love to go around. Desire for power over each other and the accumulation of more stuff, more land and more attention from others causes people to separate from the positive sprinklet qualities. This brings harmful thoughts and feelings in their futile efforts to find happiness.

    As this story unfolds, it shows what is really happening in our interactions as sprinklets and pestlets are shared. Everything you send out comes back to you like a boomerang. Those who are willing to look at their behavior earn magic star-shaped glasses. They learn the lessons to bring quality of life and the fulfilment of being loved. Teenage Dan and Peggy Jo narrate this story.

I'm going to explain how things changed on a wonderful planet called Earth.

Instead of just enjoying all the beauty and good around them, the people began to worry they would lose their blessings. When anyone had these negative thoughts, they were bothered by pesky feelings called pestlets. They're shaped like ice cubes and can make you feel boxed in with negative energy. Their energy makes you feel upset and tired.

I have **Worry Pestlet** over me right now.

A grey 'World of Worry' began to take over the peoples' thoughts and feelings. Worry Pestlet caused them to have more to worry about.

What we think about, we bring about!

Many of the people didn't protect nature
and the plants began to die.

They cut down the trees
and filled the water with trash.

Other people began to worry
they wouldn't have enough to eat
and might lose their property.

Many of them started fighting and
taking things from each other.

Some were sneaky and cheated
in games at school and on work projects.
Winning was more important
than the fun of playing the game.

They wouldn't finish if they weren't winning
and would cheat and tell lies to win.
No one likes to play games with cheaters.

When they didn't tell the truth,
a muddy lime-green Dishonesty Pestlet
hovered around them.

When someone isn't fair with others,
they know it isn't right. Guilty Pestlet makes
them feel upset about their words and actions.
They might punish themselves
and keep away blessings.

Has this ever happened to you?

**My friend Peggy Jo will tell you
What you can do about dishonesty and guilt.**

Hi! I'm Peggy Jo. I'm going to tell you what happens when you feel bad about acting bad.

If you think that you messed up,
you don't need to keep on causing yourself
problems with guilt and dishonesty.
Honesty Sprinklet is here
to offer another choice.

You don't need to stay mad at yourself.
Decide to act better next time.
Forgive yourself for things
you wish you hadn't said or done.
Then you can have 'strength of character'
and be filled with twinkling sprinklet energy.

The more sprinklets you have,
the stronger your character becomes.
You feel better and
things work out better for you too.

Some people block sprinklet blessings that others want to share with them. They worry about losing what they have
and fear bad things might happen.
They feel frozen and their actions
aren't warm and friendly.

Have you ever felt like this?

When this pesky energy gets in your way,
take in a deep breath of peaceful energy.
Think of calm, blue water. Then let go of the worry and fearful pestlet energy
as you relax and breathe out the air.

"Thoughts and feelings affect the way someone acts," said Kindness Sprinklet. Sometimes a good person can act bad. They must feel they don't have enough love, or they wouldn't behave this way.

Even when others treat you mean, you can return sprinklets to them. They need more kindness because they aren't being kind to themselves.

"Those who are acting bad can stop putting out pestlets to have more joy in their lives," said Joyful Sprinklet.

"Anything is possible," said Hopeful Sprinklet. "A pestlet can be replaced with a sprinklet as quick as snapping your fingers. The first step is to decide to stop messing up your life. Then, take a deep breath filled with sprinklet energy, and blow out the pestlet energy.
It just takes practice
to hold sprinklet thoughts every day."

"When people have sprinklet thoughts and feelings, I won't be around," complained Dishonesty Pestlet.
"If they take a deep breath of Honesty Sprinklet energy, it pushes me away."

Other pestlets may come along when you try to practice these positive changes.

Loneliness Pestlet can make you feel all alone and left out.

Have you ever let pestlets take away time to play and have fun?

Instead of doing this, you can write a story, or draw, make a craft, or go to the library.

Even if you don't have friends who can come over, you can enjoy time with yourself.

You can have fun just being in nature.

Listen to the sounds, watch the animals and take a deep breath of Joyful Sprinklet.

Dan will tell about some other upsetting pestlet energies to avoid.

When things don't seem to go
the way you want,
you could feel out of control and sad.
You can drive others away and feel lonely.

All you want to do is sit in a puddle
of red-colored depression energy,
and think about what made you upset.
It can take all your time and energy.
Instead of this, breathe in Hopeful Sprinklet
and think about what you would like
to bring into your life.

Breathe out hurtful pestlet energy.

Sometimes people get lost
in Angry Pestlet's energy.
They get madder because they keep
going over the anger in their mind
until it becomes rage.

If you stay this upset, you could say and do
things you wish you hadn't and lose control.
You can even make yourself sick.

Instead, breathe in Grateful Sprinklet energy
and feel thankful
for the good things on the way to you.

Imagine how it feels
to have these wonderful things.

I want to tell you about people
who scare others away from them.
They're called bullies.
Boys and girls can hide in bully behaviors!
They use fear to control others
for their power.

Sometimes a bully
may even act like Smug Pestlet.
They feel 'little' so they act big and tough.
Smug Pestlet is lost in fear and needs love.

If you feel this way, take in a breath
of Loving Sprinklet
and let out Fearful Pestlet energy.

Peggy Jo will tell what happened

when Pestlets took over a large group.

When the world changed, Fearful Pestlet ran the schools, businesses and even governments.

People were afraid to look at how they felt and what they were doing. They didn't understand their own feelings, much less other people's feelings. Their behavior showed little respect for themselves or anyone else. Their character got weak.

The whole world needed more sprinklets. Something had to be done about this troubling situation.

Joyful Sprinklet called a Star Council Meeting.

"We need to get people to work together instead of looking for differences and fighting."

said Joyful Sprinklet.

"They will understand how good it feels when our sprinklet energy is around them. They will see better results from the thoughts and feelings they share.

Then something shocked the whole group!

Suddenly, the door flew open!

Angry Pestlet and Raging Pestlet burst in the meeting with their mouths wide open screaming as they spoke.

"You sprinklets can't take over!" yelled Angry Pestlet.

This brought a response from the sprinklets.

"Good thoughts draw more sprinklets just like a magnet," said Honesty Sprinklet.

"We won't allow people to believe in you more than us," shouted Raging Pestlet.

Off the two pestlets went and returned shortly with all their pestlet buddies.

"I brought more pestlets. We can take over now," announced Angry Pestlet.

"By thinking about sprinklets, people replace pestlets," said Kindness Sprinklet.

"There may be more pestlets, but Sprinklet Power is stronger."

"It's up to each person to choose how many sprinklets or pestlets to have in their life," declared Joyful Sprinklet.

Then, something important happened!

Honesty Sprinklet responded by reading from the Book of Laws.

It states: "Thoughts and feelings cause behavior, which is the way someone acts. Behavior can be changed.

Each person has the power to choose to enjoy sprinklets, or cause hurt with pestlets."

"I can bring peace to people who focus on my energy," said Peaceful Sprinklet.

"What if more people ignore their anger, bury it and bring pestlets," said Depression Pestlet. They'll get back what they put out, but they won't believe it is their fault. They will never find peace that way."

Thinking peaceful thoughts turns this around," said Peaceful Sprinklet.

"I can bring joyful energy to everyone who shares sprinklet power in their thoughts and feelings," said Joyful Sprinklet.

Here are exciting ways to give joy and hope to those who want more sprinklets.

Sprinklets and pestlets are here to stay. Which will you put out and get back today? Are you choosing to make peace or problems?

"Being honest gives people greater power," suggested Honesty Sprinklet. This can bring more good things to them. Perhaps those who are truthful with themselves and accept their own feelings can earn magic star-shaped glasses. They will then be able to see the sprinklets and pestlets everywhere."

"At least they can see our affect in their lives," said Hopeful Sprinklet. "Then their magnetic sprinklet energy will get stronger and draw more friends and fun."

"I believe that people are learning that it's better to be kind-hearted to one another," encouraged Kindness Sprinklet.

"They can work together and save planet Earth!"

"They're setting up organizations and communities to help one another," added Peaceful Sprinklet. "They're giving out food and school supplies to those in need."

"The people can do it," cheered Hopeful Sprinklet.
It was amazing!
All the Sprinklets joined the chant!

"The people can do it. The people can do it!" Their energy was so powerful that the pestlets dissolved into puddles. This is what can happen when people choose sprinklet power and *strength of character.*

Book Three takes Teddy and his friend Bonnie into the amazing world of Sprinklets.

Find out what happens to Teddy when he lets the pestlets take him over.

The characters in this story find that Grateful Sprinklet and Peaceful Sprinklet lead to amazing sprinklet power.

About the Author

Patrice Joy, MA is a licensed interfaith minister and has over forty years of experience in the field of education, business, family dynamics and Integrative Health. Her educational degrees from Antioch McGregor University are a Bachelor of Arts with a double major in Health and Wellness and Human Development and a Master of Arts in Community Change and Civic Leadership. As a Reiki Master Instructor and Herbal Master, she utilizes several forms of vibrational medicine. Patrice has taught at Webster University and Forest Park Community College. She was the first woman hired in territorial sales management for the Xerox Corporation and was hostess of the TV Series entitled *The Parent's Role*. Patrice presented programs for several government agencies including CASA, Head Start, Salvation Army, Fresh Start and One Stop and presented workshops for USAF Falcon Trail Youth Camp, USAFA Family Advocacy and Older Moms Coalition. She was voted Woman of the Year in the Women's Professional Organization in 2011/2012. Her leadership skills have led her to the founding of Creative Learning Programs, Western Celebrations, Seekers of Serenity (SOS) Nonprofit and Harmonizing Health Wisdom.

About the Illustrator

Kristen Croxton graduated from Hanover College with a BA in Studio Art. She earned the Greiner Award for her senior project entitled Possible Possibilities. This innovative work remains on permanent display. Kristen wants to motivate people to realize the power of art in the healing process and to inspire people to reach their highest potential. Her main life lesson has been to follow her heart, and her life path has culminated in a unique blend of spirituality that honors the teachings of Jesus. She enjoys the psychological aspect of the Healing Feelings Series that depicts positive moral values.

Patrice can be contacted at **healingfeelings333@gmail.com**

More information is available at *harmonizinghealthwisdom*

www.ingramcontent.com/pod-product-compliance
Lightning Source LLC
Chambersburg PA
CBHW060758090426
42736CB00002B/71